Super Sophia!

by Shareen and Marcus Wilkinson
Illustrated by Nana González

OXFORD
UNIVERSITY PRESS

Jerome was sitting in the hospital waiting room with his dad, drawing a new superhero. He swapped the blue pencil for a green one and began colouring.

Suddenly, the waiting-room door opened and Mum came in.

"Your sister will be staying in hospital for a while," Mum said gently.

"How is she?" asked Jerome.

"She's doing really well," Mum replied.

Just then, a nurse came in. "You can all go in now," he said.

Jerome wasn't sure about going in. He was used to his big sister bossing him around. He wondered what it would be like, seeing her unwell.

"It's OK," Dad said softly.

Jerome took a deep breath and <u>cautiously</u> went in.

Imagine that you are Jerome, feeling <u>cautious</u> about seeing your poorly sister. How does it feel? What are you thinking?

Sophia was sitting up in the hospital bed. "Hey," she said, trying to smile.

Jerome's throat suddenly felt dry. Sophia looked so weak.

"Why don't you show Sophia your drawing, Jerome?" said Mum.

Jerome put his sketchbook on Sophia's lap. "This is Super Sprout," he explained. "He can shoot lasers from his eyes."

"This is an <u>excellent</u> drawing!" said Sophia.

Just then, the nurse came along to take Sophia's blood pressure. It was time for Jerome to go.

Can you think of another word for '<u>excellent</u>'?
Can you think of a word that means the opposite of '<u>excellent</u>'?

On the way home, Jerome thought about Sophia and what she'd said about his drawing.

At school, he often felt everyone else was better than him. Charlotte was great at football, and Adil was brilliant at science.

Jerome enjoyed art, but he thought reading was difficult. The letters seemed to move about on the page. In maths, he got some numbers back to front.

"Poor Sophia," said Mum. "It can't be pleasant being stuck in hospital. She must be bored."

"I could draw her a comic to cheer her up," Jerome suggested.

"What an excellent idea!" Mum said.

Can you think of another word that Mum could have used which means the same as 'pleasant'?

"I've got an even better idea!" Jerome said, when they got home. "I won't just do a comic *for* Sophia. I'll do a comic *about* her!"

He rushed upstairs and began to draw.

Super Sophia vs the Cosmic Crocs!

At the zoo ...

"That's not one of my crocodiles!"

Eeeeeek!

SNAP!

The zookeeper falls into the crocodile pen!

A second zookeeper arrives ...

"I don't want to get in there!"

HELP ME!

'Cautious' means being careful to avoid danger. Why is the other zookeeper being cautious here?

10

Wait! What's that?
It looks like ... a flying girl!
Super Sophia to the rescue!
Just in the nick of time ...
That is no ordinary crocodile!
NEWS!
INVASION OF THE COSMIC CROCS!
SPACE CROCODILES LAND ON EARTH

At school, another cosmic croc is on the loose ...
Arrrgggh!
Help! It's following me!
Super Sophia to the rescue!
Got you!
SWISH!
Back at the zoo ...
Into the pen with you!

At the supermarket ...

Help! A cosmic croc!

Don't worry, Dad ... I mean, *sir*. I'll save you!

Funny. She looked familiar.

That should be the last of the crocs.

Just then, an alien arrives ...

"Ah, I see you have found my pet crocs."

"Your pets? How did they get here?"

"My spaceship was on <u>course</u> for home, but I crashed. They escaped!"

"Let's get them back to your ship."

'<u>Course</u>' means the direction in which something travels. Can you imagine what happened to make the spaceship change its <u>course</u> and crash-land?

14

At the crash site ...

I don't have enough power to take off.

I can give you a boost!

WHOOSH!

That was my toughest challenge yet.

Back at the hospital …

"I absolutely love it!" cried Sophia, after she'd read Jerome's comic.

Jerome let out a sigh of relief.

"I have my own personal comic!" Sophia said. She had a big grin on her face. "I look good in a mask and cape!"

If something is personal it means that it is to do with just you. Would you like your own personal comic? What might it be about?

When they were back at home, Mum said, "Can I borrow your story to read it again, Jerome?"

"Sure," said Jerome, handing over his sketchbook.

"I just think it's so great!" Mum said, smiling.

Jerome flushed with pride.

Two weeks later …

Jerome got home from school, went straight upstairs, and slammed his door. It had been a tough day. There had been an English test, which he had found hard. Now he was fed up.

Mum knocked on the door. "What's the matter?" she asked.

"I don't really want to talk about it," Jerome said gloomily.

"Come on, get changed. I know how to cheer you up!" said Mum.

"I have a confession to make," Mum admitted, when they were in the car. "I entered your comic into a competition."

"What? But … I never win anything!" said Jerome, nervously.

"Well, we're going to the award ceremony now, so let's wait and see!" said Mum.

Do you think Mum felt guilty when she admitted what she'd done? Why/Why not?

"Sophia!" shouted Jerome, when they arrived. His dad and sister were sitting in the front row.

"We came straight from the hospital," Dad replied, smiling.

"I'm feeling loads better!" Sophia added.

"I can't believe you're here!" Jerome said. "I can't believe *I'm* here!"

Jerome saw his friends Adil and Charlotte from school. One of his teachers was in the audience, too. They all waved at him.

Jerome sat down with his family and waited nervously to find out who had won.

Eventually the head judge said, "The winner of the prize for the best comic is … Jerome!"

Everyone clapped. Jerome couldn't believe it!

Adil and Charlotte hurried over.

"Can you teach me how to draw comics?" Adil asked.

"Me too!" Charlotte added. "I'm hopeless at drawing."

"Of course I will!" Jerome said, grinning.

"What are we going to draw?" Adil asked.

"More adventures for Super Sophia of course!" Sophia cried.

Read and discuss

Read and talk about the following questions.

Page 4: What sorts of things might you feel <u>cautious</u> about doing? What makes them difficult or risky?

Page 6: What do you think is <u>excellent</u> and why? It could be your favourite food, book or animal.

Page 8: What is your idea of a <u>pleasant</u> day?

Page 14: Imagine that you had found the alien's spaceship in your school playground. What <u>course</u> would you take to fly it to your home?

Page 16: Can you imagine writing and drawing a <u>personal</u> comic for someone else? What would happen?

Page 20: Were there any parts of this book that you found hard? You could start your sentence with: *I <u>admit</u> I found ...*